TABLE OF CONTENTS

Introduction
Announcing a New Nation. 4

Chapter One
Imagining Independence 7

Chapter Two
Writing the Declaration 11

Chapter Three
What the Declaration Means 18

Chapter Four
The Declaration's Impact 22

Chapter Five
Safekeeping and Preserving the Declaration. 26

Introduction

ANNOUNCING A NEW NATION

It was a hot night in the summer of 1776. Almost everyone in Philadelphia was sleeping. But in a brick house on Market Street, a candle still burned. Thomas Jefferson was wide awake.

His quill scratched against paper. His fingers were stained with ink. He leaned over his desk, concentrating.

Jefferson was writing the first draft of the Declaration of Independence—the first step to building a new nation. The Declaration announced that the American colonies would separate from Great Britain.

For more than a year, the colonies had been fighting Great Britain. At first, the colonists didn't plan to become independent. They just wanted the British to lower taxes and give them a voice in the government. But the British refused, and the war raged on.

Thomas Jefferson

THE DECLARATION OF INDEPENDENCE

The Daring Document That Founded a New Nation

BY AMY MARANVILLE

CAPSTONE PRESS
a capstone imprint

Published by Capstone Press, an imprint of Capstone
1710 Roe Crest Drive, North Mankato, Minnesota 56003
capstonepub.com

Library of Congress Cataloging-in-Publication Data is available on the Library of Congress website.
ISBN: 9798875244643 (hardcover)
ISBN: 9798875244650 (paperback)
ISBN: 9798875244667 (ebook PDF)

Summary: The Declaration of Independence was adopted on July 4, 1776. Since then, it's become one of the most important and famous documents in American history. Young readers will learn about the Declaration's creation, influence, and meaning today.

Editorial Credits
Editor: Carrie Sheely; Designers: Nathan Gassman and Heidi Thompson; Media Researcher: Rebekah Hubstenberger; Production Specialist: Tori Abraham

Image Credits
Alamy: HISTORY CHANNEL/Album, 30, Jimlop collection, 17, North Wind Picture Archives, 16; Associated Press: File, 25, North Wind Picture Archives, 22; Getty Images: bauhaus1000, 13 (Samuel Adams signature), Edward Gooch Collection, 8, Fotosearch, 9, FPG, 21, Hulton Archive, 4, 10 (right), iStock/DNY59, 13 (John Adams, Benjamin Franklin, John Hancock, Thomas Jefferson signatures), Kean Collection, 12, Mel Melcon/Los Angeles Times, 27 (bottom), NSA Digital Archive (crown), cover, 3, 20; National Archives & Records Administration, 28; Newscom: Pat Benic/UPI, 31; Shutterstock: Christos Georghiou, 7, 10 (bottom left), 18,19, CreativeEhvan, 20 (red X), Galushko Sergey, 15, PT Hamilton, 5, Rebellion Works (arrows), 18, 19, 20, Susan Law Cain, 6, vectortatu, 27 (top right); Wikimedia: Parhamr (Declaration background), cover and throughout

Capstone thanks Mrs. Mills' 2024–2025 fifth-grade class for the feedback they gave on this book's cover design.

Printed and bound in China. 006461

More than 1 million people view the Charters of Freedom (center) each year.

Today, the original Declaration of Independence lives in a giant building in Washington, D.C., called the National Archives. It rests in a dark, quiet room called the rotunda. There, you will find three very old documents: the Charters of Freedom. These three documents were the building blocks of the United States. They are the Declaration of Independence, the Constitution, and the Bill of Rights.

You can go see them yourself, but you can't touch them! They are in special cases that protect them from damage.

DECLARATION DETAILS

WHAT?

The Declaration stated that the colonies were now independent. The fight against Britain was officially a revolution.

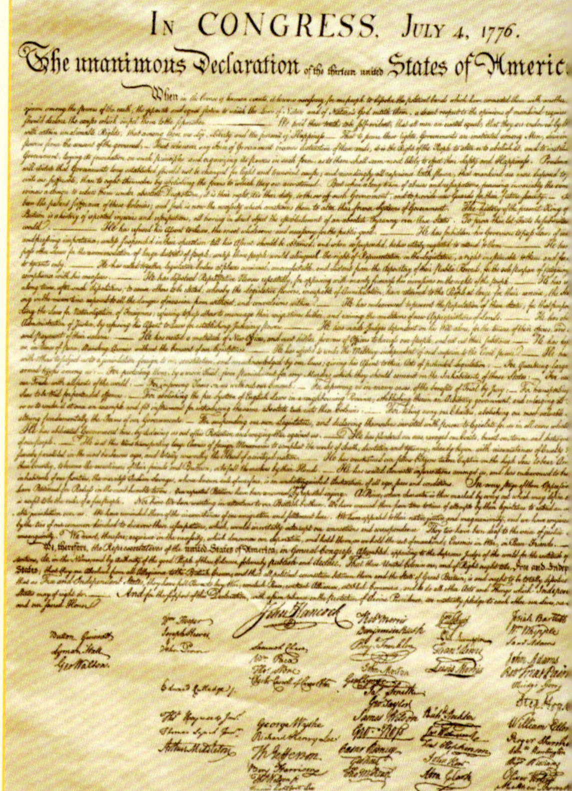

IN CONGRESS, JULY 4, 1776.

The unanimous Declaration of the thirteen united States of America

WHY?

The Declaration's creators and signers believed that the colonies had been treated unfairly. They were convinced Great Britain would keep overtaxing the colonies. The colonists didn't have elected leaders in British Parliament, the law-making part of the government.

WHO?

The Second Constitutional Congress members wrote, edited, and signed the Declaration.

WHERE?

The document was signed at the Pennsylvania State House in Philadelphia, Pennsylvania.

WHEN?

The Declaration was approved on July 4, 1776. Most leaders signed it on August 2, 1776.

Chapter One

IMAGINING INDEPENDENCE

To understand the importance of the Declaration, we have to go back to before most colonists wanted independence. It was 1770, and Great Britain had a problem. The government had borrowed a lot of money to fight the French and Indian War (1754–1763), and now they had to pay it back. The British had an idea: they would tax the American colonies to help pay the debt.

Many colonists thought the taxes were unfair. Since they didn't have anyone to speak for them in the government, they felt they shouldn't be taxed. Colonists began to protest.

One cold December night, members of a group called the Sons of Liberty and other colonists threw 340 crates of tea into Boston Harbor. They were protesting a law that gave the British East India Company a monopoly on colonial tea sales. It cut out colonial tea merchants.

The protest became known as the Boston Tea Party. Today, that tea would be worth $1.7 million.

Boston Tea Party protesters broke open crates with axes before dumping the tea overboard.

As punishment, the British passed new laws that the colonists called the Intolerable Acts. They closed the port of Boston. British soldiers were sent to Boston to control the colonists. Great Britain said that they wouldn't change the laws until Boston paid for the ruined tea. Colonists everywhere were shocked by the laws. They decided to act.

In September 1774, colonial leaders gathered in Philadelphia for the First Continental Congress. The leaders planned a boycott. The colonists would not buy British supplies until the laws changed.

The First Continental Congress also wrote down their complaints in the Articles of Association. They sent the Articles straight to King George III. They hoped that the king would stop the Intolerable Acts.

But King George refused. He thought the colonists deserved their punishment. The colonists felt betrayed.

Tension built as even more British soldiers arrived in the colonies. The colonists began gathering weapons. The American colonies and Britain were on the brink of war.

On April 19, 1775, about 700 British soldiers marched to Concord, Massachusetts. They planned to seize weapons and gunpowder. But when they got to the town of Lexington, they were met by 77 local colonists called minutemen. These highly trained militia members were able to gather quickly, and they were warned the British were coming. No one knows who fired the first shots in Lexington. The two sides battled, and the colonists won. The American Revolution had begun. When the British arrived in Concord, they were met by another group of militiamen who fought the British there.

The Battle of Lexington was fought in an open area called the Lexington Green.

Colonial leaders met again for the Second Continental Congress about a month later. Many leaders in the Congress still hoped for peace. They sent King George III another letter called the Olive Branch Petition. It said that the colonists would stop fighting if the unfair laws were fixed.

King George wouldn't even read the Petition. He was furious that the colonists had fought back against his soldiers. He announced that anyone who fought against the British was a traitor. If the colonists lost the war, their leaders could be put to death.

King George III

Chapter Two

WRITING THE DECLARATION

The leaders decided that there was no way back. In mid-June, Congress members voted to create a Continental Army and chose George Washington to lead it. The colonies would also need to declare independence. They chose a Committee of Five to write the declaration: Thomas Jefferson, Benjamin Franklin, John Adams, Roger Sherman, and Robert Livingston.

Jefferson was asked to write the draft, and he quickly got to work. Over the course of 17 days, Jefferson wrote the now famous words in a brick house where he had rented the second floor. He included similar ideas from previous writings, including Virginia's Declaration of Rights and a popular 47-page pamphlet called *Common Sense.* Written by Thomas Paine, the pamphlet supported independence from Britain. After the last word was written and the ink dried, Jefferson gave the draft to Franklin and Adams, who made some edits.

Next, the Congress read the Declaration and made changes. Jefferson didn't like the edits. He sent a copy of the Declaration to his friend Richard Henry Lee, showing which changes had been made. Lee agreed that the new version was "mangled."

One change was about enslaved people. Most of the enslaved were Black people from Africa who were kidnapped and brought to the colonies. They were forced to work in colonists' homes and on farms. They weren't paid, and they were treated horribly. Many colonial leaders owned slaves, including Thomas Jefferson. Still, Jefferson wanted to write that King George had encouraged slavery in the colonies, and that this was wrong.

But some colonial leaders wouldn't agree to the Declaration if it said slavery was wrong. With enslaved people doing work for no pay, the enslavers made more money. The Congress voted to remove that part. The Declaration was approved on July 4, 1776.

The Committee of Five worked together to create the final version of the Declaration.

KEY SIGNERS

John Adams

Jobs and positions held: lawyer, second U.S. president, first U.S. vice president

Home: Massachusetts

Benjamin Franklin

Jobs and positions held: inventor, newspaper editor, scientist, first postmaster general of the United States, ambassador to France and Sweden

Home: Pennsylvania

John Hancock

Jobs and positions held: merchant, president of the Second Continental Congress, first governor of Massachusetts

Home: Massachusetts

Thomas Jefferson

Jobs and positions held: plantation farmer, third U.S. president, second U.S. vice president, first Secretary of State

Home: Virginia

Samuel Adams

Jobs and positions held: tax collector, politician, governor of Massachusetts, leader of the Sons of Liberty

Home: Massachusetts

MAKE YOUR OWN *Paper*

The Declaration was written on a piece of parchment, which is made of animal skin. We don't write on parchment much anymore. Instead, we use paper. You can make some of your own!

You will need:

- scraps of paper (Newspaper or white paper will work.)
- bowl or bucket
- water
- blender or food processor
- piece of felt or an old towel
- parchment paper
- baking sheet

Directions:

Step 1: Tear the paper into small pieces, about 1 inch (2.5 centimeters) square.

Step 2: Put the torn-up paper in your bowl or bucket and fill with water until the paper is covered. Let this sit for at least a few hours or overnight.

Step 3: Squeeze out as much water as you can from the soggy mixture.

Step 4: Ask an adult to help you use a food processor or blender. Blend the mixture until it looks like oatmeal. (It is now pulp.)

Step 5: Spread the pulp on the felt or towel in a rectangular shape. Push down to remove extra water.

Step 6: Lay the sheet of parchment paper on top of the baking sheet. Take the paper off the felt or towel and set it on top of the parchment paper.

Step 7: Leave in the sunlight until dry.

Step 8: Draw on your new piece of paper!

MAKE YOUR OWN *Quill Pen*

Thomas Jefferson used a quill pen to write the Declaration of Independence. He even raised geese so he could use their feathers for his pens! You can make your own quill pen with only a few items.

You will need:

- a large, artificial feather with a long, hollow stem
- scissors
- pot of ink or a dark color of washable paint
- piece of paper

Directions:

Step 1: Turn your scissors at an angle. Cut the tip of the feather on a slant. It should be pointy on the end.

Step 2: Cut a small slit up the center of the pointy tip.

Step 3: Dip the cut tip of the feather into your ink.

Step 4: Sign your name with your new pen!

The Congress asked clerk Timothy Matlack to write out the Declaration. He measured, planned, and wrote the words on parchment. He left space at the bottom for the leaders to sign their names. Most of the 56 Congress members who signed the Declaration did so in Philadelphia on August 2, 1776. Seven people were not in Philadelphia on August 2 and signed the document later.

John Nixon performed a public reading of the Declaration of Independence in Philadelphia on July 8, 1776.

The leaders wanted to make sure that the words of the Declaration reached people far and wide, so they ordered copies. A printer named John Dunlap made these first copies, which were called Dunlap Broadsides.

Only two names appeared on the Dunlap copies. These were John Hancock, the president of the Congress, and Charles Thomson, the secretary. All the other names were kept private so that the British wouldn't know who signed it.

Then, in January 1777, the Congress ordered new copies of the Declaration. Washington's army was fighting well, and it seemed like a good time to share the names. This time, the printer was Mary Katharine Goddard. These Goddard Broadsides had 55 signatures. The only one still missing was Thomas Mckean's. Mckean had left before the signing to fight the British. Historians think he signed between 1777 and 1781 and that he was the last signer.

WHO WAS MARY KATHARINE GODDARD?

Mary Katharine Goddard was a printer and newspaper editor. She published a newspaper from 1774 until 1784. She made sure that the papers were delivered. Sometimes she had to pay for the deliveries herself. The Continental Congress trusted her.

The Goddard Broadsides included the 55 leaders' names plus one more. Goddard printed her name at the bottom of her copies. This was a brave thing to do. Goddard was saying that she believed in independence. If the colonists lost the war, she could be arrested or even killed.

Chapter Three

WHAT THE DECLARATION MEANS

The Declaration was an argument for independence. The words in the Declaration are old-fashioned, but their ideas are still important today. So what do some of the words actually mean?

We hold these truths to be self-evident, that all men are created equal, that they are endowed by their Creator with certain unalienable Rights . . .

What it means: All people have rights. They don't have to earn them. The word "unalienable" means that these rights cannot be taken away. Not even by the government.

. . . that among these are Life, Liberty and the pursuit of Happiness.

What it means: No one should kill or imprison anyone without a reason. Also, people should be able to do what they want. If you want to write, you can write. If you want to farm, you can farm. You can do what makes you happy.

. . . That to secure these rights, Governments are instituted among Men, deriving their just powers from the consent of the governed.

What it means: People have the right to choose their government. In Great Britain, a king ruled. Kings and queens are born into the ruling family. Instead, the colonists wanted to choose their leaders. The Declaration said that they had that right.

. . . That whenever any Form of Government becomes destructive of these ends, it is the right of the People to alter or to abolish it, and to institute new Government . . . It is their right, it is their duty, to throw off such Government, and to provide new Guards for their future security.

What it means: If a person sees a bad government, they should protest against it.

The Declaration also listed things King George III did wrong. These grievances were the reasons that the colonists felt they had to fight for independence.

Some of the grievances were:

- **The King wouldn't let the colonists trade with other countries besides Britain.**

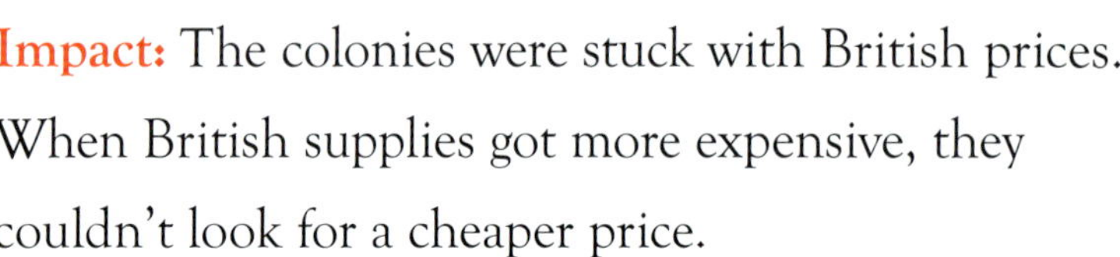

Impact: The colonies were stuck with British prices. When British supplies got more expensive, they couldn't look for a cheaper price.

- **The King fired colonial leaders.**

Impact: The people in charge worked for the British, not for the people in the colonies. No one was speaking on colonists' behalf.

- **The British Army destroyed Falmouth, Maine.**

Impact: About 1,000 people lost their homes. The Army was hurting innocent people.

WHO THE DECLARATION LEFT OUT

The Declaration of Independence said that "all men are created equal." It also said that all people should have freedom. But this did not include everyone. Some people were not treated equally or free. They were left out.

After the American Revolution, Americans still enslaved people. Enslaved people were not free until the end of the American Civil War in 1865. Even still, they did not have equal rights. Black people fought for decades against discrimination.

Indigenous people were also left out of the Declaration. They did not have freedom to live where they wanted. Colonists took much of their land. The Indigenous people never got it back.

Women could not vote until after World War I (1914–1918). They received voting rights in 1920. But even after that, women did not have equal rights.

People gather at a booth to support women's voting rights in New Jersey in 1915.

Chapter Four

THE DECLARATION'S IMPACT

Some colonists were happy about independence. These colonists supported freedom from Britain and were called patriots.

Some colonists didn't want independence. They were called loyalists. Starting in 1776, many loyalists began to leave the colonies. They didn't feel safe anymore.

King George read the Declaration, but he didn't believe that the colonists really wanted independence. He thought their leaders were tricking them. King George called the colonial leaders "daring and desperate." He said they just wanted power.

Patriots often met secretly to make plans in support of independence.

Newspapers in Britain printed the Declaration. British people read it, but they didn't think independence was the right choice. Most British people thought the colonists were ungrateful and disrespectful to their king.

TIMELINE OF THE DECLARATION

December 16, 1773: Colonial protesters throw tea into Boston Harbor.

March 31, 1774: The British government passes the Intolerable Acts.

September 5–October 26, 1774: The First Continental Congress meets.

April 19, 1775: The American Revolutionary War begins.

May 10, 1775: The Second Continental Congress meets.

June 14, 1775: The Continental Army is created.

July 5, 1775: The Second Continental Congress sends the Olive Branch Petition.

June 11, 1776: The Committee of Five are selected to write the Declaration.

June 28, 1776: The Continental Congress reads the Declaration. Changes are made.

July 2 and 3, 1776: The Congress debates the Declaration, and more changes are made.

July 4, 1776: The final version of the Declaration is approved and sent to the printer.

August 2, 1776: Most of the Continental Congress members sign the Declaration.

Benjamin Franklin took a copy of the Declaration to France, hoping that the country's leaders might help the colonies. France was an enemy of Great Britain.

The French agreed to help. They sent weapons, uniforms, money, and soldiers. With France's support, Americans won the war in 1783.

THE DECLARATION BY THE NUMBERS

1 page in the Declaration, measuring 29.75 by 24.5 inches (75.5 by 62.2 cm)

2 days the Declaration was discussed by the Congress members before they voted to approve it

27 complaints against King George III in the Declaration

35 years the Declaration hung on a wall in the U.S. Patent Office, fading in the sun

56 signers of the Declaration of Independence

86 edits to the Declaration by the Committee of Five and the Congress

250 number of years celebrated for the Declaration's anniversary on July 4, 2026

1,458 words in the Declaration (including the title and signers' names)

MORE THAN 1 MILLION annual visitors to the rotunda where the Declaration is kept

The Declaration was translated into many languages. Many people were inspired. Today, several countries, including Venezuela, Haiti, and Peru, have declarations of independence.

Americans have used the Declaration when fighting for their rights. In August 1963, civil rights leader Dr. Martin Luther King Jr. stood on the steps of the Lincoln Memorial in Washington, D.C. A large crowd was gathered there for the March on Washington. The demonstrators wanted to draw attention to racial injustice and other types of discrimination. They also wanted to support the passing of the Civil Rights Act into law. All eyes were on King as he gave his now famous "I Have a Dream" speech. In it, King talked about the Declaration of Independence, calling it: ". . . a promise that all men, yes, Black men as well as White men, would be guaranteed the unalienable rights of life, liberty, and the pursuit of happiness."

King gave his "I Have a Dream" speech in front of about 250,000 people.

Chapter Five

SAFEKEEPING AND PRESERVING THE DECLARATION

The Declaration is more than 200 years old. Throughout its history, people have tried to protect and preserve the important historical document. Where has the Declaration been and what has happened to it since it was written?

Over time, the Declaration has been damaged. Some damage may have been caused when the document was rolled up or folded as it moved around. In about 1820, son of John Adams and Secretary of State John Quincy Adams wanted an engraving of the Declaration. This would make it easier to print quality copies. People could then touch the copies instead of the original. Engraver William Stone completed the engraving in 1823. However, he may have used wet fabric or chemicals to make the engraving. The process could have soaked up ink from the original, causing fading.

IT'S A MYSTERY!

Much is known about the Declaration, but the document has mysteries too!

1. There's a handprint on the parchment. No one noticed it until 1940. How did it get there? Whose handprint is it?

2. In 1883, a photograph was taken of the Declaration, but then it disappeared. Historians have been trying to find that photo for more than 100 years!

3. Someone traced over some of the signatures on the Declaration. This made them brighter. But no one knows who did it.

The engraving of the Declaration made by William Stone

In the mid-1800s, the Declaration hung on a wall in the U.S. Patent Office for 35 years. The sun bleached the paper. The ink turned light brown, and the corners tore. In 1876, the Declaration traveled to Philadelphia. The United States was celebrating 100 years of independence. About 10 million people saw the Declaration. They talked about how worn it was, and newspapers wrote about it.

By the 1940s, the Declaration had been damaged by moisture in the air. As the humidity changed, there was softening and tightening of the document's edges. Eventually, the document tore even more.

Workers place the Declaration in a new case at the National Archives in 1952.

THE DECLARATION'S TRAVELS

1776–1783 The Declaration moves with the Continental Congress.

1783–1812 The Declaration is housed in various buildings in Pennsylvania, Washington, D.C., New Jersey, Maryland, and New York.

1814 The British invade Washington, D.C. The Declaration is stuffed in a bag with other important documents. It is smuggled to Leesburg, Virginia, for a month.

1841 The Declaration is moved to the new Patent Office Building, where it is displayed in full sunlight. This causes a lot of damage.

1876 The Declaration travels to Philadelphia for display at the Centennial Exhibition.

1877 After the Centennial, the Declaration returns to Washington, D.C. It is placed in the State, War, and Navy Building.

1894 The original Declaration is removed from public display. A copy replaces it.

1921 The Declaration comes back to public display at the Library of Congress.

1941 After the attack at Pearl Harbor in World War II (1939–1945), the Declaration moves to Fort Knox in Kentucky.

1952 The Declaration moves to its new home at the National Archives.

In 1951, experts restored the Declaration. Holes and tears were filled, and old glue was removed. The next year, the Declaration was moved to a new case filled with humidified helium. The case had a very low oxygen level, which protected the parchment from decay.

THE DECLARATION IN POP CULTURE

The Declaration of Independence is a part of America's popular culture. It has appeared in many TV shows and movies. These include the TV miniseries *John Adams* (2008) and *Sons of Liberty* (2015). The movie *National Treasure* came out in 2004. In it, there's a secret map on the back of the Declaration, and the document is stolen.

An actor in Sons of Liberty

In 2002, experts at the National Archives examined the Declaration. They made a new plan to preserve it. Its new case was made of titanium, aluminum, and glass. Light levels in the rotunda were kept low. Temperature and humidity levels stayed steady.

The case was filled with a gas called argon. Argon leaked from the case less often than helium. Sensors were installed to monitor temperature, humidity, and oxygen levels.

The Declaration of Independence holds an important place in American history, and its impact has stood the test of time. The treasured document is a reminder of the courage and strength of those who supported freedom long ago.

The cases that protect the Charters of Freedom are the result of careful work by many scientists and engineers.

READ MORE

Messner, Kate. *The American Revolution.* New York: Random House, 2021.

Micklos, John Jr. *Thomas Jefferson's Writing Desk: What an Artifact Can Tell Us About the Declaration of Independence.* North Mankato, MN: Capstone, 2022.

Miles, David. *The Side-by-Side Declaration of Independence: With Side-by-Side "Plain English" Translations, Plus Definitions and More!* Fresno, CA: Bushel & Peck Books, 2021.

ABOUT THE AUTHOR

Amy Maranville lives in Franklin, Massachusetts, with her husband, two young boys, and a vocal boxer-basset hound. She is a graduate of Smith College and holds an MA in Children's Literature from Simmons University. When she isn't writing books, she teaches composition courses at Dean College and writes historical ghost tours. Sharing stories has been a lifelong dream for Amy, and she is so proud to be able to share her work with curious young readers.